THIS BOOK BELONGS TO:

Made in United States
North Haven, CT
17 July 2023

39187733R00065